THE LANGUAGE OF GHOSTS
a debut collection by Lauren Poole

'Lauren Poole's "The Language of Ghosts" is a collection that asks its readers how language can bind us to our memories. Drenched in nostalgia and longing, these poems rip you open. They're the ancient flames of a woman angry and unafraid to sing her rage, unafraid to show us her dreams and demand answers from the darkness. These are words that get stuck in your throat and won't leave until you forgive them their edges. And by the end, you will. "The Language of Ghosts" is a collection for anyone that's felt emotions red and burning and didn't quite know how to set them down. It's raw, and cohesive, and undeniably necessary.' – Caitlin Conlon, viral poet and author of *Cavity*

'This collection is a collage of time, where the past meets the present and begs to be remembered. The Language of Ghosts confesses the things that stay and linger longer than they should, exploring the vividity of memory. Poole's poetry is powerfully impactful, her words do not hesitate to sting or caress. The Language of Ghosts takes control of the narrative and rewrites it over so the poet can finally heal.' – Melissa Jennings, author of *Dear Cassandra*

'*The Language Of Ghosts* is a patchwork quilt made of scraps of the past and present, demanding to wrap itself around you and be felt. You inexplicably simultaneously feel cold and warm. You can feel it burning in other places and itching your skin, but you simply cannot put it down. The words here are raw and potent. It is a rare thing to see so much of someone splayed out like that, and this is what poetry needs more of. These ghosts make sure their presence is known, but they're ghosts you can sit in the same room with because they are nowhere near as loud as the person they've haunted. Delving into experiences with love, heartbreak, abuse, mental health, sexual identity, and bisexuality, the author brings forth a story of healing, not in a linear form, but in a mosaic you cannot help but stand in front of and be dazed with. What you take away is this: some wounds remain a part of you forever, but they are wounds that won't always bleed, they're wounds you carry, and not wounds who carry you.' – Natalia Vela, viral poet and *Thought Catalog* writer *dedicated to my dad. if only you could see me now.*

AUTHOR'S NOTE

in her poem 'never', naiche lizzette parker wrote that
'stories don't change, we just begin to tell them
differently.' divided into 3 sections, 'preterite tense',
'imperfect tense', and 'present tense,' this book was
written partly because it has always been my dream,
but mostly as a sort of exorcism. the poems tell a story
spanning 2 years of my life, and how that story has
changed over time, depending on the rawness of the
tense it is being told from; how much it hurt, and how
much it's healing. as a writer & foreign languages
student, i'm really fascinated by the effects that
language has on us - the language we speak, the
language we hear, the words we absorb, the ways we
tell our stories. this book is called 'the language of
ghosts' because for the longest time, i have felt like
i've been communicating with dead things; toxic
relationships, internalised biphobia, sexual assault,
depression, trauma. the biggest thing i've learned since
distancing myself from these ghosts is that they are not
a part of me, as a living, breathing person. they just
live in my attic. they just scream in the night. but
they're not me. & that is why i'm telling this story:
because i'm tired of telling this story. i'm tired of
speaking in the language of ghosts. i'm tired of my
healing being prefaced by my past.
i want to note that some of the sadder topics remain in
the 'present' section - i didn't want it to be organised
from 'things are bad!' to 'now things are good!' i

wanted it to be slightly messy, because while this book chronologically explores leaving toxicity behind, putting it together reminded me that healing is not linear. healing isn't that the story has changed, as naiche wrote - it's that we're telling it differently. we're putting it behind us. the present tense is messy because i'm still living in it. i can't end my story because it isn't over yet, & i think that is the most important thing for me. burying the past tense here, so i can enjoy the flowers in the present.

i'd also like to highlight some trigger warnings in this collection: toxic relationships, suicidal ideation, depression, body image, & sexual assault.

i'm so so grateful for all of your support. thank you for being here & healing with me.

lauren x

PRETERITE TENSE

*(the immediate past, raw & messy &
bleeding. the just-crashed car, the piercing
pain in your head, the broken glass like
spilled stars all over the road).*

'when does a war end? when can i say your
name & have it mean only your name & not
what you left behind?' - ocean vuong

IN A PARALLEL UNIVERSE WHERE TIME RUNS BACKWARDS

fast-rewind through the wreckage,
all that glass unbroken and blood unspilled.
the car uncrashes
& drives into the sunset,
the roads behind us pink and gold.

fast-rewind through the day
you kissed october onto my tongue
& all the trees died around us.
the fading light,
the cardiff sky wrapped around me in a chokehold.

fast-rewind and
my dad is unburied,
my body untouched.
all of those graveyards emptying.
the taste of lightning in the bloodstream;
life surging back into summer's cold veins.

fast-rewind and the two love letters that never made it
return to my door. i realise that all along,
they should have been addressed to me.

i wipe my eyes, and the sea of beckoning gold
is just tiny railway signals, pinpricks of light
amongst the afternoon grey.

i step away from the edge of the tracks.

the sky unravels her grip on me & lets
me get on the train. for once,
my body does not feel like a heavy thing
at baggage claim.

fast-rewind and
you message me in earnest;
it's snowing in my bedroom
the first time you say hi.

i spend months ignoring your texts,
remembering everything i've been skipping through
to forget.

eventually, i reply anyway.
even knowing the ending,
i'd do it all again.

2018

it's all bloody water under the bridge.
i remember
you crashed the car.
blood everywhere,
filling my mouth,
drowning me.
an awareness of screaming.
whose? mine?
i don't even know.
my body is far away.
glass beneath my skin,
love cracking like ice at the beginning of spring,
splitting at the seams.
my clothes on the floor, your shoes gone from behind
the door.
gunshots. that clinical smell. lies in welsh.
rwy'n dy garu di. am wythnos.
picking up the phone with hands shaking
from the turmoil in my bloodstream,
what do *you* want?
yes i'm still thinking about it.
about you. her, fucking her,
in your arms bed heart,
in all the wrong places,
in all the spaces that were meant to be reserved for me.
took you a week to replace my name.
over him fuck him don't miss him

like a litany.
praying it comes true
wishing you'd come to
realise your mistake.
your love as a religion, or
trying to find faith in myself.
you probably don't think of me.
for christ's sake
get out of my head.

ALTERNATE NAMES FOR -
after danez smith

here we are again. you, car crash and me, train wreck. so you pick up after three rings and i am thinking of everything i have ever called you. like how since the day we met, your name has been my favourite. like how since the day you left, it's been lodged in my throat. how i crucified it just to bring you back to life, to unbury you in poetry. let you rent out the pit of my stomach. let you crawl inside my ribcage and live there. maybe even though i called you home, i always knew you were temporary. maybe i didn't want to believe it. or maybe i believed in a version of you that stayed. you, back-arch king. you, cherry and unholy. you, boy i named god on my knees at the altar, behind the screen, beside the sofa. you, breaking and entering everything i write. you, a crime i can't stop committing; a testimony to how easily i can be broken. you, always getting away with murder and me, never wanting to send you down, so i always take the fall. you, smiling innocently from the stand, still picking pieces of my heart from between your teeth. i tell myself the way our fault lines keep running in parallel is coincidence. the way the similarity you noticed in a few of our spotify playlists is coincidence. the way every street sign pointing to your door is coincidence. the way every name i've ever had for you being synonymous with fate is coincidence. you, a reckless

driver and me, a little too good at pretending i don't
see the stop signs. we run every red light till the city
bleeds crimson and gold. pretend we don't remember
everything we did in the back seat. here we are again.
you, headlights and me, deer: always entranced and
afraid all at once. and i missed the soft welsh lilt of
your accent. i wish i could catch it in a bottle and binge
drink it. i don't tell you this. instead, i take the piss out
of the way you pronounce 'care' and 'fuck'. the two
things we were always best at; the two things that
became our downfall. you were honey on the edge of a
blade and i never could resist your sweet taste. that is
to say i can't scrub out your name from all the
bloodstains you left in your wake. i guess your name
will always mean both love and hate, the berries and
the thorns too, both the forbidden fruit and the price to
pay. i guess it will always be embedded inside of me. i
guess it will always mean this: you, always with your
finger on the trigger, and me, always offering up my
ribs.

I AM STILL IN LOVE WITH YOU, & OTHER THINGS I PROBABLY WOULDN'T WRITE IF I THOUGHT YOU WERE READING

1. the last time i told you i loved you, i left three extra words out of the sentence.
2. you are the ocean, and the others are just seashells. empty, smooth at the edges; voices in my ear carrying me back to your shore.
3. i have introduced my lips to many hungry mouths in an effort to forget your voice, but no one listens like you do.
4. i never told you this, but in that last week, i started learning a little Welsh to surprise you. i still remember how to say *i love you*. you probably don't remember teaching me.
5. i am a language only you understand, and you are a poem i can't stop writing, even after you closed the book.
6. in a world without you, i wake up and the sky is missing. birdsong stops. there is little difference now between light and dark.
7. with nothing to look up at when i'm dreaming, for a while i stop dreaming altogether.
8. you apologise, say you're happy i'm dreaming again. for a moment, it all floods back. all that late night love and all those nightmares. all those paper thin 'i'm sorry's briefly remind me of mine:

9. i am sorry i didn't know how to write about the beauty of your spark until it burned our house down.
10. i am sorry for the way all the love poems read a little like suicide notes. all that blood and broken glass and love we don't know what to do with anymore. i am sorry i remember it all, in screaming, sharp technicolour, everything you begged me to forget.
11. i remember - vivid and crimson, every time i ever bled out for you, skin turning white, walls crying.
12. i remember - 10pm petrol station love, something you never properly made a home out of. i remember - me, your favourite gas to light and you, an ice statue.
13. i remember - digging my nails into your back as you fuck me because we really want to believe it will save us. something animal and fierce. one final, futile fight and the marks on your back to prove it. all it does is hurt. all it ever does is hurt.
14. i remember, i remember, i remember and all it ever does is hurt.
15. i guess you were right. it has to end somewhere.

LINGUISTICS
after caitlin conlon

in a language that doesn't have the word 'love' i say 'i
sent you a letter and some cat polaroids to cheer you
up' i say 'i came early for a good spot to watch you
race' i say 'i kept the bus ticket from your city' i say 'i
can't bear to wear that skirt anymore' i say 'it feels
like it's just ours' i say 'happy birthday' at exactly
midnight i say 'make a wish' and the flame goes out i
say 'i made a playlist of songs that remind me of you' i
say 'i know the one that reminded you of me by heart'
i say 'i can't listen to it anymore' i say 'everything i
write sounds like your name' i say 'i wish you were
here to read it' i say 'remember when we first met?' i
say 'and you were on that ski trip…' i say 'i remember
every word you ever said to me' i say 'that's not the
case' like you do' i say 'i miss your accent and your
little turns of speech' i say 'why don't we speak in the
same tense anymore' i say 'i'm sorry for bringing up
the past' i say 'i'm sorry' i say 'i'm sorry' i say 'i'm -'

DASHBOARD CONFESSIONAL (22 THINGS I'D TELL YOU IF YOU'D ONLY ASK // 11 THINGS I'D ASK YOU IF YOU'D ONLY TELL ME)

if you asked me, i'd tell you about how i almost died that night / spent december scrubbing blood from the christmas lights / i'd tell you i thought of you 20 minutes into the new year / that the bells sounded more like a death / than a beginning / i'd tell you that what i really want to say is i miss you is what i can't say and i know this / i do / i have to be in control this time / if you asked me, i'd tell you that yes / sometimes my finger hovers over your contact / stops in its tracks / deer in headlights or just me, suspended in all of this fear / if you asked me, i'd tell you that on the worst days, i almost hit call / but i can't / i can't keep letting you backseat drive every corner of my mind / i know this / it's so dark / and the steering wheel feels so unfamiliar beneath my shaking fingers / my white knuckles / *there's a storm coming* / (they keep saying) / *stay indoors* / (they keep saying) / but you are the safest, coldest place I know / both the thunder and the bed to hide in / both the shelter and the thing to run from / if you asked me, i'd tell you: it's so hard to call a boy home when he's got his windows boarded shut / it's easy to mistake gunshots for fireworks in the dark / either way, i keep almost crashing / i keep thinking i can see your smile seeping into the streetlights / or feel your phantom hand gripping my thigh / i'd tell you i am no stranger to your reckless swerves, your speed-limit abandon / your broken glass and torn-up hands / i am never surprised when i look down and see the bleeding. i don't think you realised any of this until you read a poem i wrote / all blood and glass and clinical smell, crash test wreckage and lies in Welsh / you were hurt, but i didn't know what to tell you / writing was the only time i was ever in the driver's seat / if you asked me, i'd tell you; honestly? i just miss being in the same car as you / i miss hearing the same songs and seeing the same sky / i'd tell you that you make me wish for a movie / for the power to fast-forward / all the days that i miss you / for a scene where the music would swell and the perspective would switch / so that i could finally stop wondering if you ever think of me / if you've cut your hair recently / how your second semester is going / for a narrator to tell me everything is going to be okay / even if i don't like what i find when i finally get to see the world through your eyes / i called the last poem for you a eulogy / as if I could ever let you die / as if the way i love you isn't synonymous with the way i can't stop digging your skeleton up / if you asked me i'd tell you about how you still follow me on Spotify / so of course i have to check your playlists sometimes / mostly just to check you're still alive / i'd tell you that i can't stop thinking that at any time / you could get hit by a car and i wouldn't even know / i can't stop thinking about how / in my mind, it always ends like this; / one of us bone-white and breathless, / bleeding out in the middle of the road. / i'd tell you that last night / i had a dream that i was outside of my body, watching myself forgive you / that even in dreams, i lay down defenceless in front of the oncoming traffic / just for a moment in the warmth of your headlights / i'd tell you that i got used to your manic driving / but still never saw the hairpin turns coming / i want to ask if you did / if you planned for it to end like this / if you ever think of me when that Alex Clare song comes on in the car / if you ever wonder what my skyline looks like now / if you'd think of me with regret if it came crashing down / *there's a storm coming* / (they keep saying) / *make sure you're not around when it hits* / (they keep saying) / but i know this / i know that i can never let you back in / that i can never know how you feel about me now / i know this / i do / i just wish i knew if you ever check my playlists, too.

-       *if you did, you'd find them littered*
        with traces of you

A COMPLETE HISTORY OF ARSON

let me tell you about the dream in which

you told me you were lying when

you said you'd stopped loving me.

or maybe

just the dream where in sleep

i get to finally stop thinking about your lies.

let me tell you about how you aren't my first thought

in the morning anymore

how i'm teaching my mind to stop

wanting to tell you anything at all

teaching my body that you're just a phantom limb;

to stop reaching for you just to find only air

because now, in your absence, i can breathe.

i would tell you what i learned

when i Googled the word 'gaslighting'

but i think you wrote the definition

and now i'm confused and spinning and unlearning

everything i thought i knew: soft

and crumbling in my hands

is love nothing more than a chopping block disguised

as an altar

disguised as a boy worth getting on your knees and
laying down your life for?

i am tired of keeping my head down

& waiting for the axe to fall

i am tired of scrubbing my blood out of your shirts

trying to wash out the red like cleansing or denial

like offering rebirth to a dead thing, & yet

still, everything you touch comes back stained & holy

& some nights i wish you'd never touched me at all.

let me tell you about how i built a new house

but sometimes i swear i can still smell the smoke

sometimes i find myself looking for fire

        waiting for fire

& i can't sleep until i've double checked the smoke alarm works

because i'm determined not to ignore any more warnings.

i am in a kind of limbo;

i am so close to uncaring

yet it is so hard not to hate you

when i'm always so fucking scared.

i spent so long in an oblivious purgatory,

always running scared to you

never realising that it was you

i should have been afraid of.

let me tell myself that i am done being afraid

but my syntax still carries the aftertaste of apology

burning my lips even as it leaves them

this is how you set fires

this is an unnamable destruction

this is tiring of thinking of myself

as destroyed

i am simply rebuilt

i am simply taking up residency in myself for a change

the paint on the walls

the new pronunciations of *home*

that don't sound like your name

what i lost in the fire

was simply a version of myself i had been taught

ever since my induction into girlhood:

the apology tucked beneath the tongue

the spaces between sentences the silences

the things we aren't supposed to talk about

the things the men do to us the things the men don't
believe

the generations of bruises and blind eyes

and hands in all the wrong places

my grandmother was tired

of the blood-dried intimacy of her husband's fists

she took the rage from years and years of silence

and she set his van on fire

which is to say that to be a girl

is to be tired and overflowing with flames

is to boil with the blood of the ancestral brave

you may have been holding the matches this time,

you may even think this means you have won

but i am cleansed & reborn

i am accepting the endings i am full of beginnings

i am soft & bright & new &

smoking at the edges

& once you have survived the wildfire

it can never burn your house down again.

IMPERFECT TENSE

*(the past getting further away in the wing
mirror, the blood starting to wash away but
still telltale traces in the carpet, still home that
was once crime scene. the bruises healing, but
still hurting when you poke them).*

'this is what the wolves taught me: the most
beautiful word is *girl.* the most beautiful part of
her body is what she did to survive.' - topaz
winters

THINGS TO SAY WHEN THEY ASK IF YOU'RE OKAY

something honest / and no, 'just plodding along' doesn't count when you haven't gotten out of bed all week / and you probably shouldn't say you're 'just hanging in there' if you aren't going to talk about all the times you've wished for a noose / it doesn't matter if you don't think you're gonna act on it / the feeling is there / it's settled at home in your stomach / and is eating away at its lining / no wonder you feel sick all the time / no wonder you feel guilty every time you eat / you don't need to apologise when you take a while to reply / you are learning to give your grief a seat at the table / you are learning to sit with it without letting it swallow you whole / even if it is almost father's day / even if it's been almost two years since your dad's last breath / even if you don't know how to say any of it out loud / even if you don't know how to hold your sadness in your mouth / without it sounding like another apology / when they ask if you're okay, tell them how being in this house is like being invisible / while the rest of the world celebrates pride, you hang yourself up in the closet before going downstairs for dinner / switch the rainbow for funeral clothes / only cry when the door is closed / only love when it won't cause distaste / it's no wonder you've gone so quiet / it's no wonder you're not hungry / when they ask if you're okay / you should swallow the knives in the back of your throat / you should finally learn to say no.

THE CARTOGRAPHY OF BIRTHPLACE

there is only one real lake in the lake district and i can
never remember its name.

still, my sentences rise and fall like hills, bending and
reaching for the light.

still, my vowels drop like stones on the water.

in some ways, my birthplace is home soil and in
others, it's foreign land.

it's an aching dream. it's Bowie on the radio, my dad's
heroic hands

pointing up at the stars. it's where the dust goes to
settle. where hearts go to slow

down. look: this is the road where i was picked up for
my first date, round the corner

from my uncle's house. i may not know all the street
names but i know what the

lights look like in the dark, i know the ground the
colour of time passing, always

familiar and unknown all at once. it's the eggshell sky
cracking itself open each

time and welcoming me home, the 'Welcome to
Cumbria' sign a dream-stained rush.

here, it's still and cold. you can hear yourself think.
look: i spent most of my

childhood here. i used to be able to name all of these
flowers.

it's sad and longing and hoping. it's always the
promise of snow, floods every year like

clockwork, a sort of baptism, another way of saying it
is okay to drown and be born

again afterwards. it's the shape of light, how it curves
and crashes and soars over the

mountaintops in shades of green and want; a kind of
heartsong. a kind of

goodbye before i knew what goodbye meant. it's that
model of the Solar System

my brother had, the one i wanted with a kind of ache
that knew only

innocence, before i knew the way of universes ripped
between the two of us,

before he became the kind of black hole no one else
would ever quite fit into. it's

the chocolate fudge cake tradition at your nanna's
favourite café, patties

that i can only get in my home county, my dad's
favourite chip shop by

the harbour. it's butterscotch angel's delight and great
open skies and conversations

with the wind. it's my sister's christening, my uncle's
fists, my father's blood:

my first taste of violence. it's train tickets always
labelled return: the kind of

happiness that weighs something. it's the same greggs
order i've been getting for

as long as i can remember, it's old photos and empty
boxes of Kendal mint cake,

it's Cumbrian inflections clinging stubbornly to my
tongue, it's every other way i

have dug your fingernails into my home county and
clung to it, even after being

dragged away. now i am muddy and made of small
graves, but my dad's name still lives

here, written in the language of stone. which is to say
that the place i began has

become a place of endings, and every new one simply
sounds like an echo of this.

there is so much empty space and none of it is mine to
take up. it is my throat

ripped open, the gulf widening, the metallic aftertaste
of war. it's no man's land.

it's choking on all of these new ways to pronounce
home; they burn and cut

and sting on the way down, salt in a long-hidden
wound. they never settle. they

never sit right in the stomach. i don't care. the hunger
for home in the ribs is

violent. it sees right through shards of glass and
swallows them anyway. my friends don't understand

why i'm like this. my tendency to let sharp things
inside me just to finally feel full.

i don't know how to tell them that it's been years since
i understood the word *belonging*.

that my birthplace is half-stranger and my new one is
full of ghosts.

they don't understand why i have made my bed on
volcanic ground, slept with one eye open.

everyone needs something to go home to.

(you just keep forgetting it's already within you).

ODE TO SCREAMING GIRLS

i wish i remembered the first time i learned that to be a
girl means to keep your mouth shut. as babies we come
out screaming, face heated scarlet, lungs full of
unbridled fire. i don't remember when the screaming
stops. how old i was when i learned that my voice is a
grenade to keep a pin in; when i first spoke up only to
be accused of exploding. each time i bite my tongue i
taste the blood of women and of course, we can't talk
about *that*. that would be *disgusting*. that would make
our bodies more than just bodies, make them
something that is real and alive before it is murdered in
an alleyway, before it becomes just another nameless
woman on the news. my key lives between my fingers
after dark because i am one of the lucky ones; my key
means safety, means home. so in isolation, it's even
harder. each day i wake up to more dead women piling
up on the pavement. i hear their locked-in screams at
night when i'm trying to sleep. but we can't talk about
that, either, without some guy shouting that *men get
abused too*, as if pointing out the abuse and murder of
women is denying male victims, as if they care about
male victims at all. they just want women to keep their
mouths shut. i can't count the amount of times i've had
this conversation with men and spat out hasty
apologies like just another symptom of fear. the
amount of times i've walked alone at night followed
by their shadows, taken three abrupt lefts and a right to

try and shake them off, my eyes glued over my
shoulder like a ghastly horror film you can't look away
from. i'm not sorry for being angry about women's
blood on the carpet, about the pretty rug placed over it
like it hasn't already seeped into the very fibres of our
houses, like it isn't already an added alarm system or
ingrained in my decoration so that (if i wear *this*
jumper), the creepy men outside the corner shop won't
shout filth at me when i'm walking home. i am tired of
women being called *hysterical* or *psycho* or *bitch* for
pointing any of this out, told to calm down, to shut up,
to be soft and pliant for the fucking or the killing,
whichever comes first. in this nightmare, he cups my
chin up with his finger like a doll, promises he is going
to make me scream. only in sex does he want me loud
and shaking - not a show of my force, but to prove his.
i don't go to his house without texting three of my
girlfriends the address. i don't go out at night in a skirt.
which is another way of saying this is *not* a nightmare.
this is not the media's tragic anomaly. this is the pulse-
cold reality women wake up to. this is the violent cost
of safety and these are the unnamed bodies that are
traded in for it. this is what it is to fear that the next
one will be your own. on a Wednesday, a man catcalls
me and i tell him to fuck off. he follows me on his
bike, promises to rape me, to cave my head in. when i
tell my male friends, they are profoundly shocked. like
harassment isn't part of the anatomy of being a
woman, something i just have to accept, like the pink

tax or airbrushing or the mind-melting fear of simply saying 'no'. like ...*maybe you shouldn't have said anything*. let me scream it from rooftops, through megaphones, let me say it loud and clear: i am tired of my outfit or lack of compliant smile shouldering the blame for his bloodlust. i am tired of feeling like prey in a land of lions, my fate and lips already sealed. i am tired of being told that being quiet is just another way of being safe, of drowning in my own silence. i would rather die trying to scream than with his dirty hand holding my mouth shut. at least that way i might be able to finish a sentence.

HIS HANDS

in the space where memory should be is
just a technicolour noise a fucked up TV static
or a scene where a girl says no and says no
and says no and tries to scream and no sound comes
out
which is another way of saying i unfollowed the boy
on instagram
but i can't stop thinking about his hands
his hands, a silent film, grey matter unasked
and unsaid his hands, huge and calloused
his hands a foreign language i never wanted to learn
but got shoved down my throat anyway his hands
a car way over the speed limit his hands
trespassing borders his hands too fast his hands won't
stop
his hands dream-stained sheets and the colour of blood
and i unfollowed the boy on instagram
because all of his photos looked right at me
with wolf-sharp eyes in shades of knowing me
in ways i never wanted
his name to be an apology i owe to my body
bent into shape & ripe with fruit wine
& unwanting & unlearning
all the ways i spent the last year carving
'your fault' into his fingerprints on my thighs & trying
to forget
his hands deaf and blind his hands reading yes

in the fearful goosebumps on my skin like braille
his hands a stuck record his hands playing over
and over in my mind his hands the reason i can't sleep
at night
his hands gone his hands gone
his hands

CO-STAR ASKS: DO YOU EVER WONDER WHY IT ALWAYS FEELS AS IF THE SEA WERE ALWAYS COMING UP BEHIND YOU?

i dream of snoozed alarm / i dream of unanswered call / i dream of messages piling up / i dream i know what to say when they ask how i'm doing / i dream of a tv show i'm not watching / a tv show i'm watching just to hear voices / i dream of the voice inside my head / i dream of *why are you so worthless* / i dream of *everyone's better off without you* / i dream of drowning it out / i dream of drowning it / i dream of drowning myself / anyway / co-star sends me my morning horoscope / asks / *do you ever wonder why it always feels as if the sea were always coming up behind you?* / yes / yes i do / i dream of the knife's edge between land and water / i dream of the water caressing my ankles / i dream of tender & breathing & glad of it / my mind is in a perpetual state of drowning / i'm just waiting for the tide to come for my body / i dream i am the girl in the movie / with the water rising in the glass box / i am just like the girl in the movie / fighting the inevitable / struggling & battling & still, the water is almost at the top / i wish i was the girl in the movie / at least then there'd be an end to all this / what i'd give for a shore to crawl onto / what i'd give for that kind of still / i learned to swim when i was tiny & now / now i'm at the mercy of the ocean / now i'm a ship halfway to wreckage / i dream of heavy arms & unforgiving waves / i dream of the phone ringing & ringing & going to voicemail / i dream of distant laughter in the next room / how light it sounds in the air / how heavy it sounds in my head / i dream in songs of ache that scale walls & beg for harmony / because they're afraid of what they'll do if they're left unheard too long / i dream of the shower / how on days like this it sounds like victory / i dream of *wow congratulations, you managed to shower. what about the million other things you need to do?* / i dream of *when are you going to do them?* / i dream of *why can't you do anything?* / i dream of *why can't you do anything right?* / i dream of the sound of sobbing against the bathroom door & avoiding eye contact in the mirror / a cacophony of hurting / & a girl begging silently for it all to stop / a girl trying to explain that on some days, depression is background noise / on others, it's deafening / either way, it's always there / always makes itself heard / i dream of a world where everything finally goes quiet / i dream of never having to wake up again

AFTER NAICHE LIZZETTE PARKER SAID 'STORIES DON'T CHANGE, WE JUST BEGIN TO TELL THEM DIFFERENTLY'

so you came up in my conversation the other day
and it hit me how foreign your name sounded.
like a language i'm losing,
it is no longer tucked under my tongue
& i'd forgotten how it tastes in my mouth.
for the longest time, it was the only one i could speak,
it was fire & gasoline & no good reason for explosion,
it was burning the roof of my mouth.
i used to curse the fire you set before i realised
that in saving myself from your wreckage,
i'd escaped with everything i need.
i guess what i'm saying is i'm not grateful for you
scorching every roof,
destroying every shred of safety i'd found.
i'm grateful i had the strength to fight through your
smoke & mirrors, to finally see myself outside
of your hazy view,
clear & refreshing as rain.
i'm grateful that where you used to be
the villain hiding in all of my stories,
now you're gathering dust on a shelf.
where you used to be fire hazard, now
you're just cautionary tale. where you
used to live between my ribs is now
just space for my lungs. i'm grateful that
without you, i can finally breathe.

MY MOTHER SAYS BISEXUALS ARE GREEDY
AND SUDDENLY I'VE LOST MY APPETITE

she is in the kitchen with her friend, spitting out my
identity before she's even had chance to chew on it,
before i've ever even let it spill from my tongue.
'like, i'm fine with lesbians, but i think bisexuals are
just *greedy.'*

greedy, she says,
and the peach pit sinking inside of me hits bottom.
i vow never to tell her about my taste for sweet,
dripping
fruit.

greedy, she says,
and i swallow all the words i've spent years sharpening
in case i ever needed to fight to be seen by her.
for the first time, i'd rather be invisible
than openly bisexual.

greedy, she says,
and i am choking on my own endless capacity for love,
swallowing my heart like chewed-up cherry pulp -
sweet and hurt and nothing anyone really wants to see.

when she shouts of me for dinner,
i tell her i am not hungry. i am sickened
by the way my name sounds in her mouth.

i do not know how to turn my identity
into something palatable enough
for her taste.

if i am greedy for loving everyone,
then so be it. let me be all jaw and no bite.
let me be soft teeth sinking into the names
of boys and girls and all the different ways
they carry their hearts. let my mouth be the
one to show them what it is to just be held.
if i am greedy, let greedy mean
open-mouthed and tender.
let greedy mean
men's aftershave and women's eyelashes
and the universal warmth of skin,
how it doesn't matter the body that wears it

because i can taste light in them all.

GRIEF IS:

crying at wedding scenes / because he'll never walk you
down the aisle / never dance with you again / grief is a
playlist of all the songs you can't listen to / all the songs
you always have to skip / the bowie, the beatles, the
prodigy / every beat that sounds like your father's name /
but isn't the same without his fingers drumming on the
dashboard / grief is the way all the music in the world
won't stop / refuses to stop / even when you're begging for
quiet / it plays outside your window / outside of *you* / you
just can't hear it the same anymore / it's distant & moving
& you have never felt so still / grief is choking up at the
sight of mars milkshakes / gathering pieces of yourself off
the floor in the dairy aisle / there's no use crying over
spilled milk or / people who are never coming back / grief
is the rest of the world blurring by in a cacophony of noise /
like existing inside a film you have no part in & / waiting
for the credits to roll / waiting to just hear the music again /
wondering if you'll ever truly hear music again / grief is
quiet and sobbing in a roomful of song / grief smiles along,
if it even makes it to the party / grief is the broken bottle on
the floor / cutting everyone's feet / until any room becomes
a minefield / grief is the elephant blocking the doorway / or
just the girl in the corner, crying again / her bleeding feet
staining the carpet / grief is the rabid animal waiting
outside for the music to stop / the girl in the bathroom
praying for the music to stop / grief is the bird on the
windowsill / dead, but singing still

A GIRL IS JUST A GIRL UNTIL

after sam payne

a girl is just a girl until she is a god / until she is arrow holes in the sky & stars clattering on the pavement / a girl is just a girl until she is holy / the shape of her body an altar / the curves of her mouth a religion / a girl is just a girl until she is sin / her hands gripping your sheets / the darkness of the closet, her smile the crack that lets the light in / a girl is just a girl until she is an awakening / until she kisses life back into your sleeping bones / her emerald eyes the only electric impulse your body knows / a girl is just a girl until she is a secret / until you can knot her name in a cherry stem on your tongue / but you can never seem to say it out loud / a girl is just a girl until she's cross-legged on your bedroom floor & telling you all the reasons she used to be insecure / & suddenly she isn't just a girl / she is acceptance / she is a kiss that doesn't taste like a prayer for forgiveness / she isn't flinching in the mirror / a girl is just a girl until she isn't 'just' anything anymore / until she gets faster / gets stronger / until the company has her name on the door / until she's built an empire one brick at a time / until she stops biting her tongue & starts swallowing fire / a girl is just a girl until she lights a match / breaks through the glass ceiling / & finally reaches the sky.

THE ANATOMY OF HEALING

so the boy's hands are rivers
and you're trying to tread water,
trying not to get swept away
because you have drowned enough times at the wrong
hands of waterfalls
to know exactly how the calm ends. to know that you
cannot get used to it.
but when the boy speaks, it's in the language of light
and you don't remember what came before that.
somewhere warmer than here, his pomegranate mouth
swallows you whole
and you forget every definition of fear you have been
clutching like cards to your chest.
and you remember what it is to not have to worry who
has the upper hand. you remember
the wanting before the knife. you are brightly and
brutally enamoured,
and still the water doesn't run red, but you keep
waiting.
you know better than eve that to know eden is to be on
the cusp of destroying it.

it would be foolish to love a mouth enough to forget its
capacity for ruination:
the world was whole and innocent as apple before we
sank our teeth into it.
and so you are made of walls and hope; a miracle of
standing, a contradiction. it's not that
you want to be afraid. just that you don't know if the
house would be safe
without the fear to guard it. and besides it has its own
room now.
which is to say the fear is as much a part of you as the
hope
that this time, there is nothing to be afraid of. which is
to say
that his name is your favourite and you are quietly
hoping it won't become
another synonym for violence.
this is the true meaning of prayer. this is what it is to
witness
war; to have it embed itself in your ribcage, take up
residency within you. to be free, yet still feel like
occupied land.

and you know too much to make a bomb shelter out of a boy again. you are just afraid that if he gets too close, he will taste the trenches on your lips. the small, quiet deaths history couldn't make space for.

this is the anatomy of healing; to some, the word 'survivor' sounds like hero. to you, it sounds like ticking. most days, you feel more time bomb than girl. which is to say that you are afraid of your battleground body. afraid it will haunt him the way it haunts you.

how seethingly, savagely human, to fear the very thing that holds you.

to return to the very place that kills you. for in dreams, you still hear the gunshots.

in dreams, you are all exit wound and hopeless prayer. but you wake up to him still, soft and beating, his body just another way of saying you are here, alive, even now. you wake up still, the warmest thing in the room, clean and breathing and

empty of ghosts.

PRESENT TENSE

(taking a deep breath and stepping out into the fresh air. driving the car into the river & swimming to safety, unafraid to leave behind anything that tried to sink you).

ALTERNATE NAMES FOR BI GIRLS
after danez smith

1. river-mouth clay
2. the push-and-pull of the moon & tide
3. *which do you like more, though?*
4. a halved, ripe peach: soft & dripping gold
5. Persephone's love of flowers & fire
6. *but if you had to pick one -*
7. the first dewy shards of dawn:
8.   unseen & honey-tongued
9. blossoms sprouting through the snow
10. the moment a cherry bursts in the mouth
11. amethyst catching the light
12. Roman baths before the ruin
13. cave walls carved with utopias of unbridled want
14. an ochre paint-by-numbers:
15. never stays inside the lines
16. stories the television won't tell you
17. straight boys' porn-soaked fantasy
18. fairy path, not crossroads
19. elixir for anyone
20. often deemed mythical
21. & real, despite it all.

NO LANGUAGE

if you'd asked me, i could've told you: there is no
language where 'no' means 'persuade me'. but you
didn't want to hear about my field of study, you just
wanted to hear the ancient hymn of my body, wanted
to kick down the doors of its church like it's your
divine right, like part of me will always owe you
kneeling. you believe in possessing, & no god can save
me from that. now i am half-temple, half-ruin, & the
worst part is i can't stop thinking *maybe it's my fault*.
no one warned me the rapist isn't always the evil man
hiding in the alley. sometimes, he's the boy at the flat
party who adds you on snapchat and makes you think
he's your friend, the boy who lives round the corner,
the boy you have to share streets with. i run into him in
the shop & forget what i am there for. i run into him in
my body & forget what that is there for, too. i say 'run
into' because all of his blood coursed in this direction;
this finish line was no accident & i am tired of my
body being a marathon route for men to conquer &
leave embedded with dirt & friction burns. i say 'run
into' because my blood is still cursing his name, mid-
way through unfreezing, meaning i am learning to stay
warm & beating in my body, & my body is learning
the art of the flight response. meaning maybe if i had
just run or fought harder or said no more firmly or
'seen the signs', maybe i wouldn't have ended up lost
& shoeless & drunk & crying, far from the end of the

road, far from any still-safe place to sleep. or maybe the problem isn't my communication. maybe some people will always run red lights, turn a 'no' into roadkill. there is no language where 'stop' means 'keep going.' & if i started running, i wouldn't stop till the sky bled at my feet.

AFTER THE ASSAULT

when i say that my body is a temple
i don't mean no one has worshipped here.
i mean i am stained glass & self-answering prayer.
i mean i made a cathedral out of my sins,
drowned every ghost that ever called me unholy.
i don't mean no one has worshipped here,
i mean *i* am worthy of worship.
i mean i have survived every burning at the stake,
i mean i have screamed & howled & crawled
my way from mud & ash to magic. i mean i
built my entire world with my bare hands
from clay & embers. look at what i've
created for myself despite every time you
tried to burn me to the ground.
i mean i have memorised my every cross & curve,
broken my body like bread at the table, fed it to
all the wrong disciples before learning that i am not
something to be consumed. i mean i made an
altar of my thighs, lit candles everywhere i didn't
want you to touch, burned away every last trace of
your
fingerprints clinging to my skin. i mean i taught
myself love like a litany: *what he did to you*
isn't your fault stop blaming yourself it doesn't matter
that you were drunk in fact it does matter that's part
of what makes it rape that's part of why it isn't your
fault
it isn't your fault it isn't your fault it isn't
i mean i reminded myself of all the times i've died
& come back again, all the battles i've survived
& all the prayers i made out of them,

all the stonings i never let harden my skin.
when i say that my body is a temple,
i don't mean no one has worshipped here.
i mean *what could be more holy than a girl*
who walked through fire & came out softer,
came out survivor,
came out heavenly
& alive?

PEACH BLOSSOM

i wasn't looking when i found you. you, early spring.
you, new breath of life. i still have a 2 second video in
my camera roll from that first night; a fragment of the
rain on the Uber window and the sea of shimmering
gold behind it. i remember how dark the world had
looked in the few weeks before that. how the city
didn't seem so hopeless that night. how suddenly, it
was beautiful all over again.

in my first few years of high school, i wrote songs
instead of poems, but i could never get the melody
quite right. i could never quite hit the right notes. but
when i wrote about love - what little i knew of it at the
time - it was always symbolised by peach trees. not for
any deep, metaphorical reason - it was something i'd
heard some girl say in the hallway that had stuck. but
for the longest time, peach trees have meant love. the
kind of love that's soft and sweet and drips down the
chin until it gets all over everything and every shard of
your life turns gold. the kind of love i didn't think i'd
ever experience.

you say that it feels like you've known me all your
life, yet it's still bright and fresh as morning dew and i
hear: in many cultures, peach trees are a symbol of
both infinity and the renewal of life. both new and
forever. they represent longevity and hope. the way

every birdsong sounds like your name. the way your
voice is a lullaby so beautiful i never want to sleep.

which is to say: i wasn't looking when i found you. but
i haven't closed my eyes since.

i guess i'd spent so long feeling like a dead thing that
when you said i was *full of life,* something inside me
stirred. i spent so long in the dark that when you wrote
a poem comparing me to the sun, it was like the first
ever dawn. which is to say that when i saw myself
through your eyes, it was like seeing myself for the
very first time. and suddenly, i was beautiful all over
again.

PORTRAIT OF US AS THOSE CHICKS
JUMPING OFF A CLIFF ON BBC EARTH

barnacle goslings have to dive over 400 feet
from the top of a cliff to find their family.
you could make a poem out of that, you said.
the baby bird's eyes bright with hope,
the way their wingspan translates distance into flight.
the way rocks are just rocks, but in flight they look like
stars
getting further and further away, the day breaking open
to welcome them home. which is another way of
saying you laugh
and suddenly it's morning,
you laugh and i put it in my back pocket for a rainy
day, you laugh
and the cliff has never felt further away.
you could make a poem out of that,
you said.
the way since i met you, jumping doesn't mean what it
used to.
the way all those miles between us become birdsong -
even when you're not beside me,
you're still my favourite thing to wake up to.
you could make a poem out of that.
the way every flight comes with a little risk.
the way some things are worth falling for.

WHAT SHIPWRECKS THE STARS:

1. how london glitters just for me and you, the streetlights dancing between our entwined hands. i'm teasing you for using google maps in your own city & your laughter is like star-foam & i am drinking the indigo night from your mouth; hours going down in seconds, joy spilling from my lips like moons, everything else eclipsed when i'm with you.

2. how there are swallows nesting in your throat; you speak in the language of feathers & want & i am curling up in the soft of your sentences, i am making my bed in your birdsong because there is nothing & no one else i'd rather wake up to.

3. how you laugh & i'm drunk & sloshing hope everywhere until even the pavement is holy ground, soaked & shining.

4. how you wash over me in waves; you smile & i am crashing into new worlds, i am shipwrecked in the stars & for once, i am not afraid; wherever i was going, i'm in the right place now.

5. how i know no matter how dark it gets, you are the sky that holds me & there is nothing i want more than to be lost in you.

KISS ME

i think we'd be okay if you'd just kiss me / even if it's for the last time / kiss me till the dreams nesting at the back of my throat take flight / till i melt into your hands of honey and silk / kiss me till Pavlopetri rises: / an underwater city opening at your touch / on the nights you hurt me i drink saltwater / and dream of your body pressed against mine, the smooth warmth of your back, your mouth / the only thing that can quench my thirst / maybe it doesn't always have to be easy / maybe i just want something to dig my nails into / so just kiss me / kiss me till your fistfuls of sky are tangled in my hair / until it's stained with starblood and want / kiss me like you're never gonna kiss me again / till the clocks hold their breath / like i never have to lose you / like it never has to end / kiss me till the gravel splits open beneath our feet and becomes holy ground once more / kiss me like we're dying / kiss me till we're still something worth dying for

IF OUR RELATIONSHIP WERE A PHYSICAL SPACE, IT WOULD BE:

1. the space between the moon & the sea - one whisper & the tide is yours
2. a waterfall: a light-dappled rush, a song of movement, loud in its wanting.
3. the valentine's card you wrote a poem about me in; the way i'm always enveloped in you
4. the space between our lips right before you kiss me; the soft coalescing of stars, the anticipation of constellation
5. that moment when the dawn breaks & light seeps through every window, golden & forgiving - i made it to another morning; the darkness doesn't last forever. *(you are a reminder that a room can always flood with warmth, even without the help of the sun)*.
6. every poem i write about you, & how they always compare you to the sky - for you are beautiful every second, & i want to know you endlessly
7. the space between a bed and its covers: liminal & dream-blurred, the colour of giggle & confession.
8. the inside of a bubble: safe & shining
9. every room in that art gallery where you kissed me
10. anywhere flowers bloom through the snow

11. the space between us means nothing: on nights like this we're bigger than all of these roads, facetime-soft & covered in stars
12. a train bound for cumbria, because you feel like coming home
13. a home we built together - a songbird in the throat, a feeling translated into physical landscape:
14. a horizon of solace, where the language we speak has no word for *alone*.

CONVERSATIONS WITH MY BODY

i knew you spoke spanish / but i didn't realise you
were fluent in the language of my skin / all rosehip &
stretch marks & freshwater springs / and yet here you
are, your fingers dripping grapefruit juice / your lips
peach-wet and soft as you come up / to kiss me
breathless / flowers blooming from the fog on the
windows / fruit growing between the sheets / i knew
you spoke spanish / but i didn't realise you were so
good with your tongue / i knew you could talk to my
body like no one else could / but i didn't realise you'd
teach it to fall / meaning i knew you were good at
eating me out / but i didn't think you'd swallow my
heart whole

- *you left me speechless from that first night. to
  this day i have no words to describe you*

BISEXUAL MAGIC

pink
i told myself i loved her in shades of green. told myself
i just wanted to *be* her. and in a way, i did. i wanted to
be the sparkle in her eye, i wanted to be the fire in her
loins, i wanted to be the spring in her step. i told
myself it was seasonal. a phase. i told myself it wasn't
real. and in a way, it wasn't. i was a pre-teen, clumsy
& raw, i hadn't figured out how my own heart fit in
my hands yet. i loved her in the way of marshmallows
and sticky lips and not knowing what to do with the
way my heart always skipped at her touch. i told
myself i didn't love her like that. i told myself i only
loved her in shades of green & envy & suddenly jade
became my favourite colour; it covered my walls,
eyelids, jumpers. i told myself i was sick, believed i
was a monster each time her eyes met mine, & i loved
her still.

blue
i didn't think i liked boys until he walked into my
english class. him with his curly hair & dirty jokes, the
way he talked with his heart open, the way he smiled
with his teeth showing. i wanted him to tear out my
heart just to prove it beat straight. i wanted him like
the children never wanted to leave narnia; like the
world inside the closet was real, like i could stay here
in the snowlight & sticky-fingered want & never have
to think of the girl again, never have to come out. i

wanted him & i wanted to be like him, heterosexual & sure. so i stayed, i ate the turkish delight, i became the witch - intent on sacrificing a part of myself, unable to see my own magic.

purple

i realised eventually that i am not a work of fiction, a truth that sometimes i think i am still learning. there are days that my pride stretches across rooftops and sings loud to the sunset, and there are days i am told my sexuality is the male fantasy's fairy story. & in a way, yes. bisexual *is* magic. bisexual is made of sugar-spun dreams & sandcastles, bisexual is both the river & the sea that holds it, & bisexual cannot be washed away.

THE ONLY HEAVEN I'LL BE SENT TO IS WHEN I'M ALONE WITH YOU

after 'take me to church' by hozier

if i wanted to make god cry
i'd tell her about your hands.
how your fingertips are like rainfall;
soft & calming & steady on my skin
until my body is shimmering
& wet with light. the flowers
dripping with gratitude,
the pavement washed of its sins.
i'd tell her i've never been a believer,
but your hands are a moonlight baptism;
each time you touch me, i am new,
my body unscarred & divine.
if i wanted to make god cry,
i'd tell her about how
you kiss hymns up my thighs
& my body is open & singing
at your touch, my body is sacred
& scorched & aching,
my body misses you so much
that each night she finds herself on her knees
praying for a little rain.

12TH JULY

in about 10 minutes, it'll be my birthday.
you're saying something about the earth taking another
trip around the sun, checking the time like a child at
christmas
& i'm helplessly in orbit of your eyes.

this weekend began much like we did:
i didn't see you coming.
you drove from the polar end of the sky
to surprise me,
like some invisible force of gravity
pulls you closer, like my smile
eclipses all of this distance.

so my 20th year begins like this: your
lips like galaxies crashing into mine,
your axis hands sending
me spinning, the arch of my back
a constellation only you can name.

so the mornings are all warm skin & skylight,
bowls of fruit in the space between our bodies,
long, slow raspberry kisses.
you tell me that i 'come looking for cuddles in the
night,'
my body crashing into yours like even in sleep,
even unconsciously, you're the moon pulling my seas

towards you until i'm a tide beneath your hands:
forever gravitating into your light,
helplessly swept away.

so i keep saying *you're not leaving* with a voice laced
with laughter, hoping if i say it enough times, it will
become true.
but of course, it isn't. you have to go
& the sky is all meteor shower,
the sky is crying stars & fire,
the sky is throwing lightning
at every road that dares to stand between us.

& of course, this isn't true either.
the sky is as blue & unassuming as any other day,
as if the world hadn't just been built in one weekend
only to crumble when your car door closed,
as if we didn't crash together to make galaxies,
only to end up as stardust & debris on the floor.

every time you drive away,
you leave a trail of stars behind you.
i'm stood at the door like in a movie,
hoping one day, there will be no more space between
us.

WHEN I SAY I LOVE MY BODY

i mean my mind is a storm
& my heart, a sapling,
my heart, bending all of this lightning
into something beautiful,
taking the thunder depression gives her
& making music out of it.
when i say i love my body
i mean i love the way you could
plant her anywhere and she'd make a garden
out of it. i mean i've spent nights in minefields
& lived to tell the tale, i mean i'm making
kinder bedtime stories out of all of these explosions.
when i say i love my body i mean today i took photos
of my tits in the sunlight just because i felt good,
danced to the weeknd in the kitchen in my underwear,
made a healthy meal & ate cherries for dessert.
i mean that i have survived every storm mental illness
has thrown at me & still, the sun glows just beneath
my skin,
still, i am growing light & fruit from all of this
darkness,
still, my body sways to the beat of every sky.
when i say i love my body
i mean i am learning to love
her for all of her hills & valleys,
how she curves & reaches for the sky, her

every stretch mark a souvenir of a storm she's
weathered,
every freckle a star forcing its way through the dark.
i mean even when i hate her, she keeps the light in my
eyes, my blood electric in my veins.
when i say i love my body, i mean i love how she is
rooted in forgiveness, refuses to let anyone shake her
down.
i mean that my mind is a hurricane while she is a
sapling -
& i am learning to love the way she grows.

FORGIVENESS

for mistaking my own body for a giving tree; for every
time winter came & i found i had no fruit left to eat.
for every name carved into the marrow that didn't
deserve the heart around it. for every uprooting; for
being cut down & torn from my home county & my
brother. for the soil that never felt like home beneath
my feet. for the blood on the carpet at christmas. for
the year i almost didn't see the lights go up. for my
father, & every definition i've rewritten of his name.
for god, or the car, or fibromuscular dysplasia, or
whatever it was that took him from me; for all the
years he won't see me grow. for everyone that's ever
taken & taken & taken from me & every time i've
extended an olive branch anyway. for allowing myself
to be harvested. for believing the only love i deserved
was seasonal & burnt orange, already halfway to
dying. for every time i fell like an autumn leaf, just to
be crushed beneath someone's feet, & for every time i
turned to rust first, killed myself before anyone else
could do it, already dead by the time i hit the ground.
for every time i reduced myself to a single leaf when
it's quite clear i'm the whole damn tree. for every time
i trembled & almost fell. for every lost bird i let make
a nest of my body. for the men who assaulted me. for
the 'friend' who didn't believe me when i said i'd been
assaulted. for the morning after & the guilt & the sick
feeling in my stomach that had nothing to do with the

vodka in my system. for every night i went out and wished i hadn't and every night i didn't go out and wished i had. for all the choices i've made over the last 20 years & all the choices i'll make over the next 20. for all the people i chose who didn't choose me. for him & him & him & her & all the songs they ruined. but most importantly, for me.

ABOUT THE AUTHOR

Lauren Poole is 20 years old, from the Lake District in the north of England, and loves tea, Minstrels, and sunsets. She has never actually been in a car crash, but metaphorically, she has had enough experience with them to last her a lifetime.

Lauren is currently based in Manchester, where she is studying for her degree in French and Spanish. She is the creator and editor of the collective anthology My Body As A Ghost Town You Won't Stop Haunting, and has been featured in publications such as War Crimes Against the Uterus, She Will Speak: Gender-Based Violence, Peach Velvet literary magazine, and more. You can find more of her work on Instagram, @laurenapoetry. This is her first collection.

ACKNOWLEDGEMENTS

I have so much to be thankful for. For my amazing friends; Harry, Emma, Aimee, Abbie, Erica, Henry, Helena, Nial, Dylon, Ben, Christian, and Chloe for their endless support.

For everyone in the poetry community – there are too many of you to name, but I appreciate all of you endlessly, especially my dear friends Caitlin, Nicole, Natalia, Diane, Kayla, Melissa, Sam, Maddie, and George.

For my brother Lewis and my sister Mia, and for my dad - for everything he taught me, and everything he would have if he'd been given the time.

And last but certainly not least, for Henry – the world stopped spinning when I met you, but it's been a whirlwind ever since.

Made in the USA
Monee, IL
17 December 2021

86127734R00039